Round and Round the Money Goes

What Money Is and How We Use It

By Melvin and Gilda Berger

Illustrated by Jane McCreary

Ideals Children's Books • Nashville, Tennessee

The authors, artist, and publisher wish to thank the following for their invaluable advice and instruction for this book:

Jane Hyman, B.S., M. Ed. (Reading), M. Ed. (Special Needs), Ed. D. (candidate)

Rose Feinberg, B.S., M. Ed. (Elementary Education), Ed. D. (Reading and Language Arts)

R.L. 2.3 Spache

Published by Ideals Publishing Corporation
Nashville, Tennessee 37214

Printed and bound in the United States of America.

Library of Congress Cataloging-in-Publication Data is available.

ISBN 0-8249-8598-2 (tr. pbk.)
ISBN 0-8249-8640-7 (lib.bdg.)

Discovery Readers is a trademark of Ideals Publishing Corporation.

It is Max's birthday.
Uncle Jack gives him a dollar bill.

Max goes to the toy store.
He gives the dollar for a balloon.

The toy store owner goes to the bakery.
She gives the dollar for a brownie.

The baker goes to Uncle Jack's pizzeria.
He gives the dollar for a slice of pizza.

Round and round the money goes.
From Uncle Jack
    —to Max
    —to the toy store owner
    —to the baker
    —and back to Uncle Jack.
Balloons, brownies, pizza.
We buy the things we want with money.

Long ago there was no money.
People grew or made everything they
needed.

Then things started to change.
People did only one kind of work.
Farmers farmed.
Hunters hunted.
Weavers made cloth.
Woodcutters chopped wood.

Now people needed other things.
So they traded
    —potatoes for cloth
    —fish for meat
    —or firewood for animal skins.

But trading wasn't always easy.
Suppose a farmer wanted a new coat.
And a weaver wanted a cow.
"A cow for a coat?" said the farmer.
"That's not a good trade.
"A cow is worth more than a coat."

Then some people had an idea.
They said, "Let's trade with shells!
"We all like shells.
"And shells have value.
"They are hard to find."

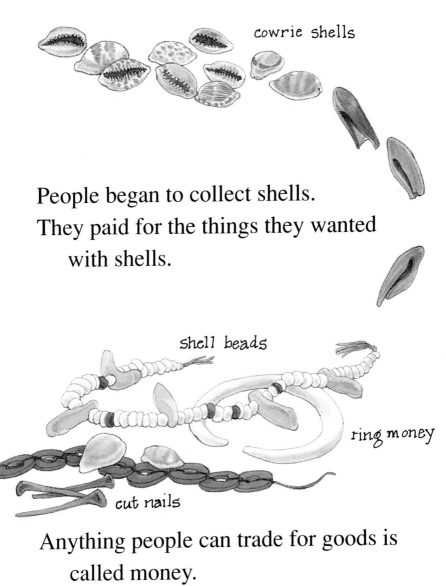

cowrie shells

People began to collect shells.
They paid for the things they wanted
with shells.

shell beads

ring money

cut nails

Anything people can trade for goods is
called money.
Shells were one of the first forms of
money.

9

Now the farmer could buy the coat
    with his shell money.
He could give the weaver three shells for
    the coat.
And the weaver could buy the cow
    with his shell money.
He could give the farmer ten shells for
    the cow.

The ancient Chinese used shells for
    money.
But other peoples used other things.

Native Americans used beads made
into wampum belts.

clam shell
beads

Africans used lumps of salt.

reed band
keeps salt
together

Mexicans used beans.

cacao beans

On the island of Yap, people used
huge stone rings.

hole for
carrying
on pole

On the Santa Cruz islands, they used
red feathers.

11

Many also began to use metal as money.
The metal had many shapes and forms.
Metal money was shaped like

—an axe

copper
money axe
from Mexico

Ancient
Chinese
bronze
hoe-shaped
coin —
6th century
B. C.

—a hoe

—or even a knife.

Ancient Chinese
bronze knife-shaped
coin — 3rd century B.C.

Metal money was good for a few reasons.

It did not wear out.

It could be made in any size.

The bigger it was, the more it was worth.

Everyone wanted gold and silver.

Those metals were most rare.

So they had the most value.

coins

standard weights

Wall paintings show Egyptians
weighing precious metals
against standard weights

13

Workers in a country called Lydia made
the first coins.
Today Lydia is known as Turkey.
Lydians started making coins about
2,600 years ago.
It was about the time of the first Olympics
in ancient Greece.

Coins were a new kind of metal money.
The coins from Lydia were called *staters*.
They were made of a mixture of gold
and silver.

The staters were all about the same size.
Each one was marked with a lion's head.
This showed that they were money.

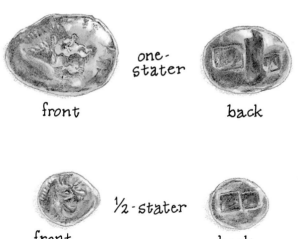

one-
stater

front   back

½-stater

front   back

The idea of using coins for money
spread far and wide.

Soon the Chinese stopped using shells.
They began to make coins of iron.
But the iron coins were big and heavy.
People found them hard to carry around.

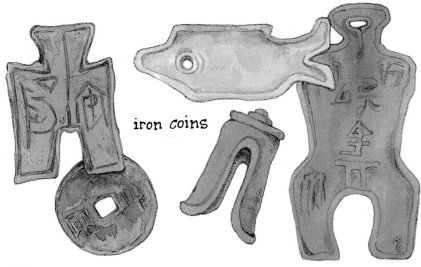

iron coins

Then, about 1,400 years ago, something new began in China.

People left their big coins in the stores.

The storekeepers gave them notes.

The notes showed the number of coins each person left at the store.

In time, the Chinese treasury began to print paper notes.

The treasury is the part of government which makes money.

The treasury gave each note a certain value.

The notes became China's money.

Today every country prints its own paper
money.

Each country calls the money by a
different name.

In England it's the *pound*.

In France it's the *franc*.

In Germany it's the *mark*.

In Italy it's the *lira*.

In Spain it's the *peseta*.

18

In Mexico it's the *peso*.

In Canada it's the *dollar*.

In Japan it's the *yen*.

In Taiwan it's the *dollar*.

In Australia it's the *dollar*.

Paper money in the United States is
   called the dollar.
All dollars are the same size and color.
But they have seven different values—
   $1, $2, $5, $10, $20, $50, and $100.

In the past the United States also had
   dollars of greater value—$500,
   $1,000, $10,000, and $100,000!

Dollar bills are made at the Bureau of
Engraving and Printing in
Washington, D.C.
Engravers cut designs into steel plates.
Other workers put the designs on
printing plates.

Printers set the plates into a printing
press.
Press operators print new dollar bills.

Dollar bills are very hard to copy.
The government doesn't want anyone
　　else to make them.
Engravers put hundreds of thin lines
　　into each design.
Printers use ink with secret chemicals.
Printers even use special paper.

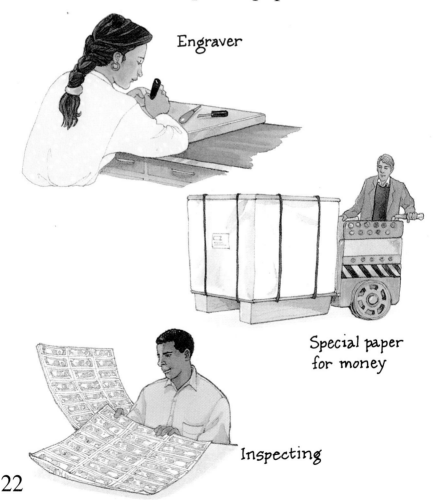

Engraver

Special paper
for money

Inspecting

Look very closely at a dollar bill.

You'll see tiny red and blue threads in
the paper.
Other invisible marks are there too.

Dollar bills pass from person to person.

For about a year, the dollars go round and round.
By then the bills are wrinkled and worn.

Banks send the old bills back to
    Washington, D.C.
The treasury department burns the old
    bills.
Every day they burn many millions of
    old dollars.

U.S. Treasury

The U.S. Mint in Washington, D.C.,
makes coins.
They make pennies, nickels, dimes,
and quarters.

In the past they also made half dollars
and silver dollars.
Coins last much longer than dollars.

The coins are a mixture of metals.
Pennies are made of copper and zinc.

Copper bar

Nickels, dimes, and quarters are
made of copper and nickel.

raw nickel pieces

An artist carves the
    coin's design.

Then a worker puts the design on a steel
    punch.
Others mix the metals together.
They form them into bars.
A machine presses the bars into flat strips.
The strips are as thick as the finished
    coins.

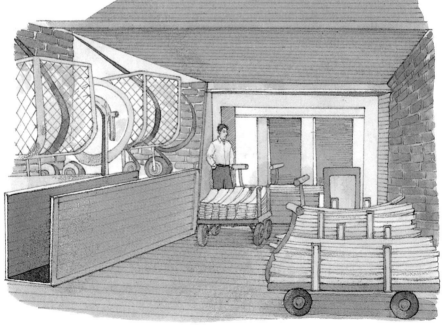

Another machine cuts out "blanks" from
  the strips.
Blanks are the same size as the coins.
But they have no design.

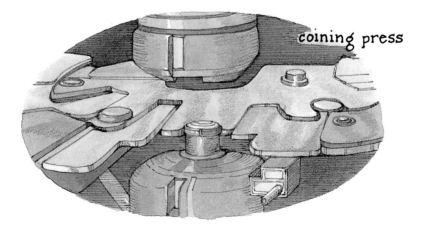

Big machines press the steel punch on
  the blanks.
The punch stamps the design on the coins.

coining press

Get a shiny new nickel and a magnifying
  glass.
Look under President Jefferson's collar.
Do you see the letters "FS?"
They stand for Felix Schlag.
He's the artist who carved the head of
  Jefferson on the nickel.

Look under President Roosevelt's collar
   on the dime.
Do you see the letters "JS?"
They stand for John Sinnock.
He carved the head of Roosevelt.

People make money in different ways.

They work and earn wages.

They sell things.

They receive money as gifts.

They get an allowance.

32

Suppose you want to earn some money.

You can mow lawns, shovel snow, or baby sit.

You can walk dogs, weed gardens, or deliver bundles.

You can sell old, used toys, games, or books.

Can you think of other ways to earn money?

It's fun to spend the money you earn.
You can buy something you need.
But always ask a grownup first.

Or you can give money to charity.
Charities help people who are in need.
They may be very old or homeless.
They may be children who are poor or
sick.

You can also give money to
—churches or synagogues
—hospitals or animal shelters
—orchestras or museums
—and lots of other groups.

It's also fun to save your money.
You can save for something special.
You might want

    —a new CD or video

    —a bike or ice skates

    —a book or computer game

    —or a jacket or sneakers.

Start saving your money at home.
Find a good, safe place to keep it.

After awhile, bring your money to a
bank.

Banks today do what stores in China
    did long ago.
They will hold your money.
They will give it back to you when you
    ask for it.

Banks will also give you back a little
  extra money.
The extra money is for letting them
  hold your money.
We call the extra money "interest."

Suppose you put $100 in the bank.
A year later you want your money back.
The bank will give you back your
  $100—plus interest.

During the year, the bank will use your
money.

It will lend the money to other people.

People borrow money from banks

—to buy a house or car

—to pay for college or go on a trip

—to buy a new TV or computer

—or to buy anything that costs more
than they have.

People who borrow money must pay it
   back.
And they must pay back a little extra
   for using the money.
The extra money they pay back is also
   called interest.

Suppose someone borrows $100.
A year later the person pays it back.
The bank will ask for $100—plus
   interest.

Suppose you have $100 in the bank.
You decide to buy a new bike.
The bike costs $75.

There are a few different ways to pay
for the bike.
You can take $75 out of the bank.

And you can give the store owner $75 in
dollar bills.
This is called paying with cash.

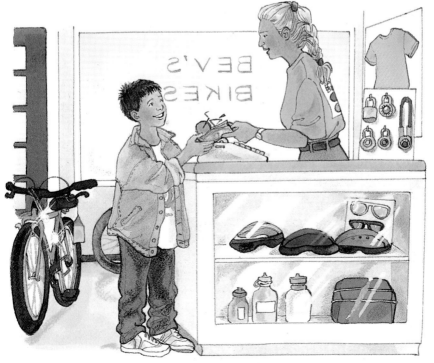

Or you can ask an adult to write a check.
The check tells the bank to pay the
    store owner $75.
You give the check to the store owner.
The store owner takes the check to the
    bank.
And the bank gives the store owner $75.

Or an adult can use a credit card.

Using a credit card is like borrowing money.

The adult shows the store owner the card.

The store owner fills out a slip.

He or she sends the slip to a credit card company.

The credit card company sends the store owner $75.

The credit card company sends the adult a bill for $75.

He or she pays the credit card company $75.

Cash, check, or credit card.

Either way, you get the bike.

Either way, the store owner gets $75.

Earn money.

Save money.

Spend money.

Give the money to charity.

Round and round the money goes.

Index